Recipes from Wales

113 TRADITIONAL WELSH RECIPES

JOHN JONES

'Recipes from Wales'
© JOHN JONES PUBLISHING LTD 1994
First edition, March 1994
New edition, March 1996

Text originally published under the title of 'A Welsh Welcome'
by the Wales Gas Board in 1953. Revised edition 1957
Re-published by John Jones Cardiff Ltd, 1979
New edition, JOHN JONES PUBLISHING LTD, March 1984

Cover: 'Market Day in Old Wales' by Sydney C. Vosper.
Reproduced with thanks and acknowledgements
to the National Museum of Wales, Cardiff.

ISBN 1 871083 60 5

GRACE BEFORE MEALS

O Dad, yn deulu dedwydd
Y deuwn, a diolch o'r newydd,
Can's o'th law y daw bob dydd
Ein lluniaeth a'n llawenydd.

Amen

Benedic Domine nos et haec tua dona quae de tua
largitate accepimus per Christum Dominum nostrum

Amen

Distributed by: The Welsh Books Centre, Llanbadarn,
Aberystwyth, Dyfed.
Published by: JOHN JONES PUBLISHING LTD
Reg. Office: Barclays Bank Chambers, St Peter's Square
Ruthin, Denbighshire.
Printed by: Dinefwr Press Ltd., Llandybie, Dyfed.

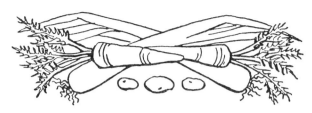

CAWL CENNIN
LEEK BROTH

A lump of salt bacon
Potatoes
Carrots
Leeks

Parsley
Cabbage
Oatmeal and water

Place the bacon in boiling water and with it the root vegetables, cut up small. Boil for about 1½ hours.

Remove the bacon and add the leeks, together with some finely shredded white cabbage. When these two vegetables are cooked, add a tablespoonful of chopped parsley and serve. The cawl can be thickened by adding two tablespoonfuls of oatmeal mixed into a paste with cold water. This could be added at the same time as the leeks.

In the old days this made a two-course meal – the cawl itself was the first and the meat and vegetables the second course. Any cawl left over was reheated and drunk for breakfast the next day and was known as "cawl ail-dwym".

CAWL HASLET

1 *lb. pig's liver*
1 *lb. onions*

1 *lb. potatoes*
Pepper and salt to taste

Cut liver in small pieces, slice onions and prepare potatoes. Allow the liver and onions to simmer in three pints of water for 1½ to 2 hours. Add potatoes, simmer for another half-hour, season with salt and pepper. Strain and serve very hot.

CAWL MAMGU
GRANNY'S BROTH

2 lb. best end of neck (Welsh lamb)
1 small swede
½ lb. carrots
1 lb. potatoes
2 large leeks
1 oz. parsley
½ oz. flour
Salt and pepper

Put the meat into the saucepan, cover with cold water, add salt and pepper, bring slowly to the boil and skim carefully. Add the carrots (cut in half), the swede (sliced) and the white of the leeks, and simmer gently for 2 to 2½ hours. Add the potatoes (cut in four) and continue to simmer for another 30 minutes. When the potatoes are almost cooked, thicken with flour and little water. Lastly, add the green of the leeks and parsley (chopped) and simmer for further 10 minutes, and serve in basins while hot.

CAWL MAMGU TREGARON
TREGARON GRANNY'S BROTH

1½ lbs. bacon
1 lb. shin beef
1 white cabbage
½ lb. carrots
half a small swede

½ lb. parsnips
1 lb. potatoes
1 large leek
Oatmeal to thicken

Use a large saucepan and see that all the meat and vegetabes are covered by water. Boil ingredients, except leek, together and leave to simmer for as long as you wish. Put in leek ten minutes before serving and let the cawl boil.

4

OYSTER SOUP FROM GOWER

Melt 2 ozs. of butter in a pan and rub into it about 1½ ozs. of flour. Pour on to this some well flavoured mutton broth. (The broth should be flavoured with onions, mace and black pepper.) Bring to the boil and allow to simmer and thicken for about 15 minutes.

Strain and pour over the required quantity of oysters, already bearded.

TEISEN GOCOS
COCKLE CAKES

Six-pennyworth of cockles. Stand overnight in water sprinkled with oatmeal. Wash well and boil. Dip in thick batter and fry a spoonful at a time in hot fat.

PASTAI GOCOS
COCKLE PIE

Cook one quart of cockles in a cup of water. Line sides of pie-dish with pastry thickly rolled. Put a layer of cockles in the bottom of the dish. Sprinkle with chopped chives or young spring onions, then a layer of bacon cut dice size. Repeat these layers until the dish is full. Pour in liquid in which the cockles were boiled, adding pepper. With strips of pastry make a criss-cross over pie. Cook slowly until pastry is done. This pie is delicious served hot with new potatoes or cold with mixed salads and dressing.

Oven Control, Mark 6

PASTAI BRENIG
LIMPET PIE

A quantity of limpets, already cooked
¼ lb. of fat or streaky bacon
2 hard-boiled eggs
1 onion
Some bread dough or short crust pastry

Line deep pie dish with thinly rolled-out dough or short crust pastry. Fill dish with alternate layers of limpets, bacon cut up in cubes, sliced eggs and sliced onion. Add seasoning and a little of the limpet liquor. Cover with dough or pastry. Bake in a hot oven for ½ hour, and then more slowly for another ½ hour.

Oven Control, Mark 7 and then Mark 5

BARA LAWR
LAVER BREAD

Wash the seaweed well to remove all the sand. Boil for hours. Mix with fine oatmeal and form into small cakes. These are fried, preferably in bacon fat, and are excellent for breakfast.

Laver is a kind of edible seaweed which can be bought in Swansea Market and elsewhere along the western coast, already prepared.

This can be offered with bacon for breakfast or with mixed grills.

WAYS WITH LAVERBREAD

(It is a tradition not to use an iron pan or metal spoon. Use wooden spoons or silver fork or spoon, and an aluminium saucepan.)

1. Heat tablespoonful of butter in pan, put in laverbread and a squeeze of lemon-juice, and serve on hot, buttered toast.
2. Mix small quantity of laverbread with squeeze of lemon-juice, add a few drops of olive-oil, pepper and salt and spread on fingers of toast, crackers or crisp bread for a savoury or hors d'oeuvre.
3. Thick slices of bread fried in bacon fat spread with hot laverbread, topped with chopped ham or bacon, pepper and salt, and if liked a few drops of onion juice.
4. Serve piping hot laverbread mixed with a squeeze or two of seville orange juice as a vegetable accompaniment to Welsh mutton.
5. Coat flat cakes of laverbread with oatmeal and fry in bacon fat.
6. Mix laverbread with fine oatmeal, then coat with oatmeal and fry in bacon fat.
7. Eat laverbread cold with vinegar, as is the custom in Cornwall.

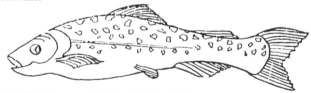

BRITHYLL A CIG MOCH
BAKED TROUT AND BACON

Line a pie dish with thin slices of fat bacon. Split and clean the trout and place on the bacon. Sprinkle with chopped parsley, pepper and salt. Cover and bake for about 20 minutes.

Oven Control, Mark 4

7

SWPER SCADAN
HERRINGS FOR SUPPER

1 lb. medium sized herrings
1 large cooking apple
1½ lbs. potatoes
1 salt-spoonful made mustard
1 salt-spoonful made sage
1 large onion
½ oz. margarine
Pepper and salt to taste

Clean herrings, bone and divide into fillets. Spread the insides with the mustard, sprinkle with salt and pepper and roll up.

Peel and slice potatoes and onion; peel, core and slice apple. Put half the potatoes into a greased pie-dish, add apples, then onion and the herring rolls. Sprinkle with the sage. Cover with remainder of apple and potatoes and seasoning and half fill the dish with boiling water.

Put little nuts of margarine on top, cover, and bake in a moderate oven for an hour; remove cover and leave in the oven for another half hour.

Oven Control, Mark 5

TEIFI SALMON SAUCE

The salmon should be washed in salted water, dried carefully and cut into slices. Mix ¾ of a pint of melted butter with a glass of port, a little ketchup and one boned anchovy, in a pan over a low flame. Pour this sauce over the salmon, place fish in a covered dish in a fairly hot oven, leaving it to bake for about ¾ hour.

Oven Control, Mark 5

FFOWLIN CYMREIG
WELSH CHICKEN RECIPE

Chicken (one or two)	*2 large leeks*
½ lb. bacon (cig mochyn)	*Bunch of mixed herbs*
½ lb. carrots	*Pepper and salt*
1 oz. butter	*Stock*
1 oz. flour	*Dripping*
1 small cabbage	

Young birds need not be used for this dish. Truss them as for boiling. Cut the bacon, leeks, and carrots into dice. Put them into a casserole with the butter and fry for a few minutes, stir in the flour until it thickens and browns. Place the chicken in the thickened sauce. Wash and cut up a small cabbage and put it into the casserole with the chicken, add a bunch of herbs, leeks and sprinkle in pepper and salt. Add ½ pint of stock, put some small lumps of dripping or butter on the bird, cover, and simmer for 2 or 3 hours. When serving, make a bed of the cooked cabbage on a dish and place the bird on it. Garnish with the carrots and pour the liquor over the cabbage.

9

SPICED BEEF

12 *lb. of flat ribs*	¼ *oz. pepper*
½ *lb. salt*	¼ *oz. cloves*
¼ *lb. Demerara sugar*	¼ *oz. allspice*
1 *oz. of saltpetre*	¼ *oz. mace*

Bone the meat; mix the salt, sugar and the rest of the ingredients together. Place the meat in a deep dish and sprinkle over with the dried mixed ingredients. Turn the meat every day for a fortnight. At the end of the fortnight wash well and roll up and tie. Place in a self-basting tin or casserole with some beef dripping and roast in a moderate oven for four hours. Turn out on a meat dish, cover with a plate and place a weight on top. Beef treated in this way is very tender and tasty. Serve cold with a salad.

WELSH LAMB PIE

1½ *lb. neck lamb*
Teaspoonful finely chopped parsley
Small bunch young carrots
Pepper and salt
Short crust

Bone the meat and cut into small pieces, clean and cut carrots into thin rounds, put layer in bottom of dish, then meat, parsley and pepper and salt. Repeat until all is used; cover with water, 2 in. from top. Cover with pastry and brush over with milk. Bake two hours in moderate oven. Boil the bones, one onion, pepper and salt 1½ hours, and when pie is ready strain and pour into pie. Serve hot or cold. This is a very old and good dish.

Oven Control, Mark 6 for 20 minutes then down to Mark 4

VEAL STUFFING

To 6 *ozs. bread crumbs allow*
3 *ozs. lean ham or bacon*
4 *ozs. suet*
2 *teaspoonfuls of minced parsley*
1 *teaspoonful of thyme*
2 *eggs*
Salt and pepper

Shred up the ham or bacon, add the chopped herbs, suet and bread crumbs and well blend; season and add a little grated nutmeg. Beat up the eggs and bind the mixture.

PASTAI BRAIN BACH
ROOK PIE

It was usual to have a "rook shoot" in May, when farmers shot many young rooks.

Only the meat from the breasts of the birds was used, and this was put in a pie dish lined with short pastry. Chopped bacon, chives, and thyme were added, the meat seasoned, and a little stock added. The pie was covered with pastry and baked in a moderate oven.

Oven Control, Mark 6

11

KATT PIE

A traditional dish made on Templeton Fair Day, 12th November, for at least 200 years.

1 *lb. flour*	*½ lb. currants*
½ lb. suet	*½ lb. sugar (brown)*
good pinch salt	*Salt and pepper*
½ lb. minced mutton	

Make hot-water pastry by boiling suet in water, add to flour and salt, stirring well with wooden spoon. When cool make into pies about 4 ins. in diameter. Arrange filling in layers – mutton, currants and sugar, salt and pepper; cover with a round of thin pastry. Bake in hot oven 20 to 30 minutes. Eat hot.

Oven Control, Mark 7

FFAGOD SIR BENFRO
FAGGOTS

1½ *lb. pig's liver*
4 *ozs. breadcrumbs*
3 *ozs. suet*
2 *large onions*
1 *or 2 teaspoonfuls sage (chopped)*
2 *teaspoonfuls salt*
¼ *teaspoonful pepper*

Mince raw liver and onions into bowl. Mix with bread crumbs, suet, salt and pepper and sage thoroughly. Form into small balls.

Bake in a moderate oven for about 30 minutes; pour boiling water into tin to form gravy.

This savoury dish was popular after pig-killing in Pembrokeshire 60 years ago.

Oven Control, Mark 5

GLAMORGAN SAUSAGES

1 *egg*
a little very finely chopped onion
a pinch of mixed herbs
a pinch of mustard
Pepper and salt
5 *ozs. bread crumbs*
3 *ozs. grated cheese*

Divide egg yolk from white, mix all dry ingredients and bind with yolk of egg. Divide into small sausages and roll in flour. Dip each into white of egg, then roll in breadcrumbs and fry in pork fat. Serve with creamed potatoes or chips.

STWNS RWDAN A IAU

This is a popular North Wales dish using liver, onions, swedes and potatoes.

Cut the liver into slices and fry till dark brown. Roll in seasoned flour. Fry the sliced onions and rub them also in seasoned flour. Place the liver and onions in a saucepan or a casserole, cover with water, and simmer slowly for 2-3 hours.

Serve with potatoes and swedes well mashed together into what is known as a "stwns".

It is a popular custom in Wales to mix potatoes into a "stwns" with various vegetables, e.g.:
Stwns pys – potatoes and peas mashed together.
Stwns ffa – potatoes and broad beans mashed together.

A favourite dish in the old days was a "stwns" with buttermilk poured over it!

PASTAI GWNINGEN
RABBIT PIE

Pastry	*2 teaspoonfuls chopped parsley*
1 rabbit	*Nutmeg*
½ lb. beef steak	*Pepper and salt*
¼ lb. cooked ham	*Stock*

The rabbit should first of all be soaked in salt water for 1½ hours, then jointed and placed in a pie dish together with the ham and steak, cut up into small pieces; sprinkle with chopped parsely, pepper and salt and nutmeg, add the stock, and cover with pastry. Bake slowly for 1½ hours.

Or

The rabbit, etc., can be cooked for an hour and a quarter in a covered pie dish and then covered with pastry and cooked in a hot oven for 20 minutes till brown.

FFEST Y CYBYDD
THE MISER'S FEAST

This dish was very popular in Carmarthenshire about 100 years ago. Then it was made in a saucepan. Nowadays it can be made equally well in a casserole. Cover the bottom of the saucepan or dish with peeled potatoes and a sliced onion, with a little salt. Cover with water and bring to the boil. When the water is boiling, place on top of potatoes and onion a few slices of bacon or a piece of ham. Replace the lid and allow to simmer till the potatoes are cooked, when most of the water will be absorbed. The miser was supposed to eat the potatoes one day, mashed up in the liquid, keeping the slices of bacon to be eaten the next day with plain boiled potatoes.

TATWS RHOST
HOT POT

This is similar to Ffest y Cybydd. Fill a casserole with alternate layers of Welsh bacon, sliced onions and thickly sliced potatoes. Add pepper and salt. Cover with a lid and cook slowly for two or three hours. Remove lid for the last 20 minutes to brown the top layer of potatoes.

Oven Control, Mark 3

WELSH STEW

Beef
Potatoes
few carrots
Onions
A small swede (if liked)
Small piece of home-cured bacon (if liked)

Cut up the meat into small pieces; place in a saucepan with less cold water than you would use for soup; simmer for about one hour before adding carrots, onions, swede (all cut up small); continue to simmer for about ½ hour. Finally, add potatoes (cut up) and seasoning. This dish must be cooked slowly, and not allowed to get too dry. Serve very hot with pieces of bread.

POTEN BEN FEDI

2 *lbs. potatoes*   1 *onion*
1 *cup minced cooked meat*   *knob of margarine*
1 *rasher bacon*   *spoonful wheaten flour*

Boil potatoes, then mash, adding the knob of margarine and spoonful of wheaten flour. Chop up rasher of bacon and onion and fry them, then add bacon, onion and minced meat to the mashed potatoes.

Add salt and pepper, then mix all together and turn into a greased pie dish and bake in a moderate oven for about 20 minutes till top is golden brown.

Oven Control, Mark 6

TEISEN DATWS
POTATO CAKES

Potato cakes were popular in North Wales during the last century.

1 *lb. cold cooked potatoes*
3 *tablespoonfuls flour*
2 *tablespoonfuls brown sugar*
1 *teaspoonful baking-powder*
¼ *teaspoonful cinnamon*
Milk to mix to a fairly stiff consistency

Put mixture into a greased tin, and put in a fairly hot oven to start with, then lower the temperature, and leave the cake to bake for two hours.

The cake can be eaten hot or cold, sliced and buttered.

Oven Control, Mark 7, then after 20 minutes down to Mark 4.

TEISEN DATWS
POTATO CAKES

1 lb. boiled potatoes
4 ozs. flour and 1 teaspoonful baking-powder
1 egg
1 oz. butter or margarine
1 tablespoonful sugar
Pinch of salt

Melt the butter and mix in all the ingredients. Roll out about one-inch thick. Bake either on a girdle or in a hot oven for 20 minutes.

Oven Control, Mark 7

TEISEN NIONOD
ONION CAKE

Peel some potatoes, slice them and place them in a layer on the bottom of a well buttered cake tin. Sprinkle a layer of finely chopped onion on the potatoes and small lumps of butter or margarine. Repeat these two layers till the tin is full – adding pepper and salt to taste. The top layer must be of potatoes, on which some butter is spread. Cover with a lid or a plate and bake for one hour in a moderate oven. This cake can be eaten with hot or cold meat.

Oven Control, Mark 5

LEEK PASTY

¾ lb. flour
6 ozs. lard and a pinch of salt
1 teaspoonful of baking-powder

Rub well together, mix with cold water into a paste. Cut in two, roll out thin to fill a large dinner plate, take two or three handfuls of leeks, wash, cut up finely and lay over first layer of paste, put a few strips of fat bacon on top of the leeks, add pepper and salt to taste, add an eggcupful of cold water, add the other layer of paste and cook in a hot oven till done.

Oven Control, Mark 6

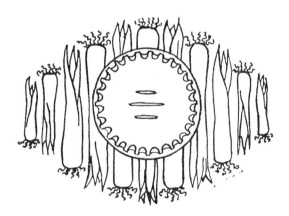

POTATO CHEESE CAKES FILLING

½ lb. mashed potatoes   *¼ lb. sugar*
¼ lb. currants   *¼ lb. butter*

Mix all well together. Line patty tins with pastry and fill with mixture. Bake until golden brown.

Oven Control, Mark 6

PASTAI BWMPEN

1 *moderate-sized vegetable marrow*
1 *cupful of currants*
1 *cupful of sugar*
1 *dessertspoonful of vinegar*
½ *teaspoonful of nutmeg*
Short-crust pastry

Peel the marrow and take away the centre. Cut the remainder into cubes. Line a pie dish with short-crust pastry. The put a layer of cubes into it, layer of sugar, layer of currants, sprinkling of nutmeg. Continue the layers in this order until the pie dish is full. Lastly, add the vinegar. Cover with a layer of pastry and bake in a moderate oven until the fruit is cooked.

Serve hot or cold. *Oven Control, Mark 6*

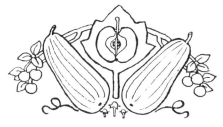

POTEN BWMPEN

10 *ozs. short-crust pastry*   *few cloves*
vegetable marrow   *pinch ginger*
few crab apples   *slat, little water, milk*
½ *cupful of sugar*   1 *egg*

Line a fairly large pie-dish with short-crust pastry. Peel and slice the marrow and apples. Put them in layers in dish; sprinkling between each layer cloves, sugar, salt and a little water – top off with remaining apples and a little ginger. Cover pie; decorate with pastry leaves. Brush over with the beaten egg and milk, and bake in a moderate oven for one hour.

Oven Control, Mark 6

TOCYN Y CARDI

1 tablespoonful each of rolled oats and plain white flour
2 tablespoonfuls of milk
1 teaspoonful of baking-powder and a pinch of salt

Mix all dry ingredients together. Make into small cakes and fry in bacon fat. Serve with fried bacon.

TROLLIES BLAWD CEIRCH

½ lb. of fine oatmeal   *2 ozs. suet*
2 ozs. self-raising flour   *2 ozs. currants*
Pinch of salt

Mix all dry ingredients well together; then mix to a firm dough with water or milk. Make into trollies about the size of an egg and boil in any soup for 45 minutes.

Delicious with boiled bacon.

CAWS POBI
WELSH RAREBIT

4 ozs. grated cheese
3 tablespoonsful milk
1 oz. butter
Pepper and salt (mustard if desired)
Slice of toast

Place cheese and milk in saucepan and melt slowly. Add pepper, salt and butter. When piping hot pour it over the toast and brown under the grill. A little beer is sometimes added to the mixture.

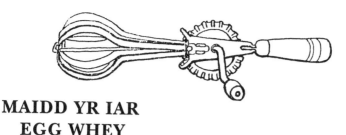

MAIDD YR IAR
EGG WHEY

Thick slice bread
1-2 eggs
About ½ pint of milk
Little ginger, nutmeg and sugar

Break a thick slice of bread into a saucepan. Add the well-beaten eggs and the milk, then the ginger, nutmeg and sugar. Allow to stand on top of the stove till it sets. It must not be allowed to boil. Instead of the old method of using a saucepan, it can be cooked just as well in a cool oven, as for egg custard.

MAIDD WY

Break an egg into a basin, add a pinch of salt and two teaspoonfuls of sugar. Beat well, then add very slowly about a gill of boiling water. Be sure to stir briskly at the same time. Cut up some bread (as for bread and milk) and add to the liquid. Let it stand for a few seconds, and just before serving add two tablespoonfuls of draught beer. It makes a wonderful night cap.

PWDIN REIS DYDD SUL
A SUNDAY RICE PUDDING

Boil 1½ ozs. of rice in about ½ pint of milk till soft, and add 1 oz. of sugar.

Mix another ½ pint of milk and 1 oz. of sugar with two beaten eggs and add to the boiled rice.

Pour the mixture into a pie dish lined with puff pastry. Bake for abut ½ hour till the custard is set and the pastry is browned.

Oven Control, Mark 6

21

PWDIN REIS MAMGU

2 *ozs. rice*
2 *ozs. demerara sugar*
Pinch salt
½ *pint water*

1 *pint milk*
½ *teaspoonful nutmeg*
1 *oz. butter*
1 *or* 2 *eggs*

Simmer rice in water until grains are swollen.

Add butter, sugar and milk, nutmeg, and pinch of salt, and cook gently for about two hours, stirring frequently. Remove from heat and beat in egg yolks. Just before serving add stiffly beaten whites of eggs.

Serve with jam or honey.

PWDIN WATCYN WYNNE

10 *ozs. breadcrumbs*
8 *ozs. chopped suet*
3 *ozs. sugar*
3 *eggs*
Pinch of salt
Juice and grated rind of two lemons

Mix well and put into a basin. Cover and boil three hours. It should be served with a sauce made as follows:

Melt some butter with brown sugar adding grated lemon peel and nutmeg and a glass of sherry or Madeira. Make hot, but do not boil, and serve immediately.

Substitute half a wineglass of lemon juice for the sherry if preferred and make up balance with golden syrup.

PWDIN ERYRI
SNOWDON PUDDING

8 *ozs. suet*
6 *eggs*
1½ *ozs. cornflower (or rice)*
6 *ozs. sugar (brown if possible)*
8 *ozs. breadcrumbs*
4 *ozs. raisins (stoned)*
6 *ozs. lemon marmalade*
Grated rind of 2 lemons
Pinch of salt

Mix all the dry ingredients (except a handful of raisins), beat the eggs and add. Pour into a greased basin, into which the remainder of the raisins have been spread. Cover and boil for 1½ hours. Serve with white sauce, or on special occasions with wine sauce made as follows:

Boil 1½ ozs. of sugar and the rind of half a lemon in about a wineglassful of water for about 15 minutes and then remove the rind. Beat about half a teaspoonful of flour into an ounce of butter and stir into the water. Add one-and-a-half wineglasses of sherry, Madeira or white wine and serve really hot.

TROLLINS

6 *ozs. self-raising flour*
2 *ozs. suet*
2 *ozs. currants*

Pinch of salt
A sprinkle of nutmeg

Mix ingredients with milk to a stiff dough. Cut into four or six pieces. Mould into rounds and flatten to about three-quarters of an inch thick. Dip each piece in flour, then drop one by one into a saucepan of boiling water. Cook about 20 minutes.

Serve hot, with a spoonful of demerara sugar and a nut of butter on each. Trollins make a nice change from milk puddings after dinner.

PANCOSEN FAWR

6 *ozs. self-raising flour*
2 *ozs. to 3 ozs. sugar*
1 *egg*
¼ *teaspoonful bicarbonate of soda*
Milk

Mix flour, sugar, and bicarbonate of soda together. Beat egg and add to the flour, adding milk to make a fairly thick batter.

Using a frying pan cook four slices of home cured Welsh ham. Keep in a hot dish until required. Pour the batter into the hot fat and cook both sides until golden brown. Cut into four portions and serve hot.

PWDIN AFAL   PWDIN EFA
APPLE PUDDING OR EVE'S PUDDING

2 ozs. plain flour
1 oz. sugar
1½ ozs. butter

2 eggs
½ to ¾ pint milk
Stewed apples – Vanilla

Melt butter in a saucepan, stir in the flour and add the milk a little at a time. Bring to the boil to make a smooth sauce. Pour into a bowl and add the sugar, a few drops of vanilla and the egg yolks. Then fold in the stiffly beaten egg whites.

Grease a pie dish, and cover the bottom with a layer of stewed apples. Pour the mixture over them and bake for three-quarters of an hour.

Oven Control, Mark 6

CREMPOG LAS
AN OMELETTE

½ lb. flour
1 teaspoonful chopped parsley and chopped shallot
2 eggs
Pepper and salt and a little milk

Mix and cook like pancake, beating the batter really well. Spread with butter and eat hot.

PONCO

Make a batter with:

2 teacupfuls of flour
½ teaspoonful of baking-powder
Milk, and a pinch of salt

After frying bacon or ham, leave the fat in the pan and pour the batter into it. Fry until brown on both sides. Can be eaten with bacon and/or fried tomatoes, or with a hot meal of meat and vegetables.

CRAMPOETHAU
CRUMPETS

1 lb. flour
2 or 3 ozs. of brown sugar
1 egg
1 pint of milk
½ teaspoonful of bicarbonate of soda

Place the dry ingredients together in a bowl. Beat the egg well and add the milk to it. Add the liquid gradually to the flour, etc., and mix carefully till smooth. Cook on a bake-stone as pancakes. Butter and sprinkle with sugar. To be eaten hot.

PICE'R PREGETHWR
PIKELETS

4 ozs. flour   *3 ozs. butter or margarine*
2 eggs   *½ pint buttermilk or milk*

Rub the butter into the flour, beat the eggs and mix into a batter, beating well with a wooden spoon. Allow to stand overnight if possible. Bake on a girdle and eat hot and well buttered.

CREMPOG GEIRCH
OATMEAL PANCAKES

Recipe No. 1

6 *ozs. fine oatmeal*
1 *lb. white flour*
½ *oz. yeast, mixed in warm milk, and a little sugar*

Mix the two flours, and add the yeast and sufficient milk to make a thin batter. Cook as pancakes and eat hot, spread with butter.

Recipe No. 2

1 *lb. flour*	1 *egg*
½ *lb. oatmeal*	1 *oz. yeast*
1 *teaspoonful salt*	2 *teaspoonfuls baking-powder*

The oatmeal should be soaked in water overnight. Put flour and baking-powder in a basin and add the yeast mixed with a little milk. Add the well-beaten egg and then the oatmeal water. Care must be taken not to add too much oatmeal water – the mixture should drop off a spoon, but not be too thin. Cook as pancakes, spread with butter (and sprinkle sugar on them if desired). These can also be reheated and eaten with bacon.

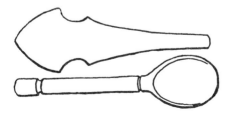

CREMPOG
WELSH LIGHT CAKES OR PANCAKES

6 tablespoonfuls flour
2 tablespoonfuls sugar
2 or 3 tablespoonfuls of sour cream if available
Pinch of salt
½ teaspoonful bicarbonate of soda and 1 tablespoonful cream of tartar dissolved in water
2 or 3 eggs
Buttermilk or milk to mix

Make into a batter, beating till bubbly with a wooden spoon. Bake on a hot girdle of frying pan, using very little fat. Serve hot with butter. The old way was to make large pancakes, spread them with butter, pile them on a plate and cut into quarters.

PANCWS LLAETH SUR
SOUR MILK PANCAKES

½ lb. self-raising flour
2 ozs. butter or margarine
3 ozs. sugar
¼ teaspoonful salt
A pinch of ground nutmeg
1 level teaspoonful of bicarbonate of soda
2 eggs
½ pint of sour milk

Rub butter into flour. Add salt, ground nutmeg and sugar. Mix well together. Beat eggs and add to the flour. Dissolve the bi-carbonate of soda in the sour milk. Stir until it effervesces and add to the mixture. Drop from a dessertspoon on to well-greased bakestone and bake light brown on both sides. Serve hot, piled high and buttered.

BARA BRITH
CURRANT OR SPECKLED BREAD

There are several recipes – two ar given.

With eggs – a very old recipe.

3 lbs. flour
¾ lb. brown sugar
¾ lb. lard or butter or mixed
2 or 3 eggs
1 lb. raisins
1 lb. sultanas
1 lb. currants and ¼ lb. candied peel

1 oz. yeast
½ teaspoonful pudding spice
1 teaspoonful salt
Milk to mix

Mix yeast with warm milk. Rub the fat into the flour and mix the dry ingredients. Make a well in the centre and add the yeast. Mix into a soft dough, then cover and leave in a warm place fo 1½ hours to rise, till twice its original size. Turn on to a floured board, place in greased tins, stand again in a warm place for about 20 minutes and bake in a moderately quick oven for 1-2 hours. When cold, cut and butter as for ordinary loaf – thin slices with plenty of butter!

Oven Control, Mark 6

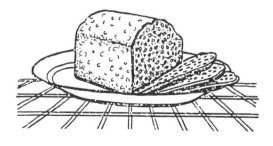

BARA BRITH
CURRANT OR SPECKLED BREAD

Without eggs.

2 *lbs. flour*	6 *ozs. currants*
1 *oz. yeast*	4 *ozs. candied peel*
8 *ozs. brown sugar*	1 *teaspoonful salt*
8 *ozs. fat*	*½ teaspoonful pudding spice*
6 *ozs. sultanas or raisins*	*Warm milk*

Mix yeast, a little sugar and warm milk. Rub fat into the flour, add the dry ingredients. Make a well in the centre and add yeast. Knead into a soft dough. Cover and allow to rise to twice its size in a warm place, for 1½ hours. Turn on a floured board, put into greased tins and bake in a moderate oven. Slice thinly and butter.

Oven Control, Mark 6

OLD WELSH GINGERBREAD

This was the gingerbread sold at the old Welsh fairs.

¾ lb. flour
½ teaspoonful bicarbonate soda
1 teaspoonful cream of tartar
6 ozs. demerara sugar
¼ lb. butter
2 ozs. chopped candied peel
6 ozs. black treacle warmed slightly and mixed
* with 1 gill of milk*

The bicarbonate of soda and cream of tartar are added to the flour and well sifted. Rub butter into the flour, add sugar and peel, mix with the treacle and milk. Bake in a greased tin for 1½ hours.

Oven Control, Mark 3

BARA CARAWE
SEED LOAF

1 *lb. self-raising flour*
1 *teaspoonful salt*
½ *tablespoonful carraway seeds*
1 *oz. sugar*
2½ *ozs. margarine (or butter)*
1 *egg*
¼ *pint milk or milk and water*

Sieve flour and salt into basin. Rub in the fat and add the other dry ingredients. Mix to a soft dough with egg and milk (previously well-beaten together). Put in a greased bread-tin. Bake for one hour in a moderate oven.

Oven Control, Mark 5

SEED CAKE

200-year-old Welsh recipe.
We feel Mrs. Beeton would have approved this recipe.

2½ *lbs. flour*
2 *lbs. refined sugar*
12 *ozs. carraway seeds*
2 *lbs. butter or margareine*
4 *teaspoonsful orange flower water*
10 *eggs*
½ *lb. candied peel*

Cream butter and sugar, add eggs one at a time with flour alternately, then add orange flower water, carraway seeds, candied peel. Put in tins when the oven is ready. Let the fierceness of the oven be over before you set in the cake for fear of scorching it.

Oven Control, Mark 3 for one hour then down to Mark 2,
and finally Mark 1 till cooked

TEISEN SINSIR
GINGER CAKE

4 *ozs. butter*
1 *lb. flour*
2 *ozs. sugar (brown)*
1 *lb. treacle*
1 *oz. candied peel*
1 *oz. ground ginger*
2 *eggs*
1 *teaspoonful bicarbonate of soda*
1 *teacupful of milk*

Heat together the treacle, butter and sugar. Mince the peel and add the beaten eggs. Put dry ingredients in a bowl, add the beaten eggs gradually and then the treacle, etc., and milk as required. Pour into a shallow tin, well greased, and bake for ¾ hour in a moderate oven.

Oven Control, Mark 4

CINNAMON CAKE

½ *lb. flour*
4 *ozs. sugar*
4 *ozs. butter*
Yolk of one egg and whites of two
½ *teaspoonful baking-powder*
1 *teaspoonful cinnamon*
Jam

Mix the baking-powder with the flour and rub in the butter. Add the sugar and cinnamon and the yolk of the egg to make a stiff paste. Roll out and place on a shallow tin or plate – as for making a plate tart. Cook "blind" in a hot oven. Allow to cool and spread with jam. Beat the whites of egg until stiff, fold in a little sugar, spread on jam and return to a cool oven to set.

Oven Control , Mark 6
Oven Control, Mark 3, for meringue

TEISEN SIR FÔN
ANGLESEY CAKE

Recipe No. 1

> 10 *ozs. flour*
> 4 *ozs. lard*
> 3 *ozs. sugar*
> 1 *egg*
> ½ *teaspoonful bicarbonate*
> 1 *tablespoonful of treacle*
> *Pinch of mixed spice and ginger*
> 4 *ozs. dried fruit*
> 1 *cup of milk*
> *Pinch of salt*

Cream the sugar and fat. Mix in the egg and add the remainder of the ingredients, having dissolved the bicarbonate in the milk. Bake in a greased tin for about ¾ hour in a moderately hot oven.

Oven Control, Mark 5

Recipe No. 2

> 3 *teacups of flour*
> 1 *teacup of butter*
> 1 *teacup of sugar*
> 3 *teaspoonfuls of baking-powder*
> 2 *eggs*
> *Milk to mix*
> *A little dried fruit*

Rub the butter into the flour, add sugar, baking-powder and well-beaten eggs and milk if necessary – it must be kept fairly stiff. This is enough to fill two sandwich tins. Bake for 30-40 minutes. Cut in half, spread with butter and eat hot.

Oven Control, Mark 5

TEISEN BOETH
HOT CAKE

4 ozs. plain flour
2 ozs. sugar
2 eggs (or 1 egg and a little milk)
2 ozs. butter or margarine
Good teaspoonful of baking-powder

Cream the butter and sugar, mix the flour and baking-powder and add the beaten eggs and flour alternately. Divide into two sandwich tins and bake in a hot oven for 12-15 minutes. Have some butter already softened and spread as thickly as possible on the two halves. Then put the two halves together. Sprinkle the top with sugar. Currants and raisins can be added if desired. This is an excellent cake – when butter is plentiful.

Oven Control, Mark 6 or 7

SLAPAN

½ lb. flour
1 or 2 ozs. sugar
2 ozs. dried fruit
2 eggs
A little milk if necessary
A pinch of bicarbonate and a pinch of baking-powder

Rub the butter into the flour, then the well-beaten eggs and the remainder of the ingredients to make a thick batter. Place in spoonfuls on a bakestone and cook on both sides. Eat while hot, split and buttered.

SLAPAN SIR FÔN

1 *lb. plain flour*   ½ *lb. fat*
½ *lb. caster sugar*   *Teaspoonful baking-powder*
3 *eggs*   ¼ *lb. currants*
Pinch of salt

Rub fat into the flour, add salt, sugar, currants and eggs well-beaten. Beat well. Then stir in lightly the baking-powder and a little milk if necessary. Grease the bakestone with lard, put mixture out in spoonfuls.

Bake both sides. Serve hot.

TEISEN GRI

½ *lb. flour*
2-3 *ozs. fat (butter, margarine or lard)*
1-2 *ozs. sugar*
1 *egg (optional)*
¼ *teaspoonful salt*
½ *teaspoonful bicarbonate of soda*
1-2 *ozs. currants*
Buttermilk or milk

Rub the fat into the flour and salt. Add the dry ingredients and mix well. Add the milk to make a soft dough and turn on a floured board. Shape into a round and roll to about ½ in. thick. Bake both sides on a hot girdle. Should be eaten well buttered.

CACEN-CRI

1 *lb. flour*
4 *ozs. butter (or margarine)*
4 *ozs. lard*
1 *egg*
1 *teaspoonful salt*
2 *ozs. fruit*
1 *teaspoonful baking-powder and a little milk*

Sieve flour, baking-powder and salt together, rub in fat and mix into stiff paste with egg and milk. Roll out thinly and cut into rounds. Bake on a bakestone. Butter, but do not split. Serve hot.

THREE RECIPES FOR TEISEN LAP

TEISEN LAP (1)

1 *lb. flour*
4 *ozs. lard*
4 *ozs. margarine*
2 *heaped teaspoonfuls baking-powder*
7 *ozs. sugar*
8 *ozs. currants*
3 *eggs*
A *little nutmeg*

Rub the fat into the flour and add the dry ingredients. Add the well-beaten eggs and enough milk to have a soft mixture. Bake in a moderate oven, using a shallow tin.

Oven Control, Mark 5

TEISEN LAP (2)

1 *lb. flour*
4 *ozs. fat*
4 *ozs. brown sugar*
4 *ozs. mixed fruit*
½ *teaspoonful of spice*
½ *teaspoonful of bicarbonate of soda (dissolved in milk)*
1 *egg*
½ *pint of buttermilk or sour milk*

Rub fat into the flour, add sugar, fruit, spice; mix well together. Add the beaten egg and the milk and beat to a soft dough. Divide the dough and roll out to an inch in thickness; bake on a bakestone or hotplate; time about 15 minutes, when nicely brown one side, turn them over.

TEISEN LAP (3)

This cake should be baked in a Dutch oven before an open fire to make it in the traditional Welsh way but the results are just as good if you bake it in a well greased oblong tin (spread the mixture thinly) in a moderate oven for about 35 to 40 minutes.

1 *lb. flour*
1 *teaspoonful baking-powder*
Pich of salt
A little grated nutmeg
4 *ozs. butter*
4 *ozs. sugar*
4 *ozs. dried fruit (sultanas and currants)*
3 *eggs*
½ *pint milk (sour milk is delicious)*

Sieve flour, baking-powder, salt and nutmeg. Rub in lightly butter, add sugar and fruit, whisk the eggs, and add to mixture. Gradually add the milk, mixing all with a wooden spoon. The consistency should be soft enough for the batter to drop from the spoon.

Oven Control, Mark 5

37

BERFFRO CAKES

(A kind of Short Cake or Sugar Cake)

1 *oz. sugar*   2 *ozs. butter*
3 *ozs. flour*

Mix well by hand, roll out fairly thin an cut into rounds. In Anglesey, where Berffro (short for Aberffraw) cakes originated, it is the custom to make each round with a scallop shell. Bake in a moderate oven and sprinkle with sugar.

Oven Control, Mark 3

PICE AR Y MAEN
WELSH CAKES

Recipe No. 1

8 *ozs. flour*
½ *teaspoonful of baking-powder*
2 *ozs. margarine*
2 *ozs. lard*
3 *ozs. sugar*
2 *ozs. currants*
¼ *teaspoonful mixed spice*
Pinch of salt
1 *egg*
A little milk

Rub fat into flour. Add dry ingredients, then egg and milk. Mix into a stiff paste – as stiff as for short pastry. Roll out, cut into rounds and bake on a girdle.

PICE AR Y MAEN
WELSH CAKES

Recipe No. 2

1 *lb. plain flour*
1 *teaspoonful baking-powder*
¾ *lb. butter or margarine or mixed with lard*
¼ *lb. currants*

Mix with sweet milk, roll out, cut into rounds and bake on a girdle. Sprinkle with sugar.

TEISEN TINCAR
TINKER'S CAKE

1 *lb. flour*   ½ *lb. fat – margarine or butter*
6 *ozs. sugar*   *A little grated apple (cooking)*
A pinch of salt

Mix all the ingredients into stiff dough; roll out and cut into small rounds. Bake on a bakestone as for Welsh cakes.

DINCA FALA

10 *ozs. self-raising flour*
5 *ozs. butter*
5 *ozs. demerara sugar*
1 *lb. cooking apples*

Rub fat into flour, and add sugar and apples peeled and cut into small pieces. Mix with enough milk to make a fairly stiff mixture.

Cook in greased tin.

Oven Control, Mark 6 for ½-hour

TARTEN AFALAU
APPLE TART

All kinds of plate tarts with pastry top and bottom are popular in Wales – apples, rhubarb, gooseberries or mixtures of any kinds of fruit in season can be used.

TARTEN EIRIN
PLUM TART

Filling
1 lb. plums, cut in half and stone removed
4 small apples sliced
4 ozs. of sugar for sweetening, and a little water

Pastry
The pastry is spiced – using 8 ozs. flour and 4 ozs. fat, and
½ oz. sugar and a little water; with ¼ teaspoonful of
cinnamon and a pinch of mixed spice

Line a plate or shallow tin with half the pastry. Fill with fruit, cover with sugar and add a little water. Cover with the rest of the pastry and bake for 45 minutes.

Oven Control, Mark 6 for 20 minutes then down to
Mark 4 to finish

40

TEISEN PLANC
PLANK PASTRY

Make the pastry in the usual way, using half fat to flour. Roll it out very thinly and cut out two rounds using a plate to measure the rounds. Spread one round with jam and place other on top. Bake on a bakestone, not too quickly. Turn over and bake the other side. Sprinkle with sugar.

BARA CEIRCH
OATCAKES

3 tablespoonfuls hot water
½ tablespoonful bacon fat
4 tablespoonfuls medium oatmeal
Pinch of salt

Melt the fat in the water, then sprinkle the oatmeal on to it, kneading well by hand. Roll out very thinly on a board floured with oatmeal. Cut into large or small rounds as desired. Bake on a moderately hot girdle or in a thick frying pan, for about ten minutes. Allow to harden in a warm place. In the old days it was customary to leave the oatcakes to harden on a "diogyn" – literally a "sluggard" – in front of the fire. Oatcakes must be pressed and rolled out as quickly as possible. It is not advisable to mix too many at the same time.

TEISEN FÊL
HONEY CAKE

4 ozs. honey
1 teaspoonful cinnamon
4 ozs. brown sugar
1 egg
½ lb. flour
½ teaspoonful bicarbonate of soda
4 ozs. butter or margarine
Castor sugar for dredging
A little milk

Sieve together flour, cinnamon and bicarbonate of soda. Cream butter and sugar. Separate the egg yolk from the white. Beat the yolk into sugar and butter, then add the honey gradually. Stir in flour with a little milk as required, and mix all together lightly. Whisk the egg white into a stiff froth, and fold into mixture. Half fill small patty tins with the mixture; dredge the top of each with castor sugar. Bake in a hot oven for 20 minutes. When ready sprinkle a little more sugar.

Oven Control, Mark 6 or 7

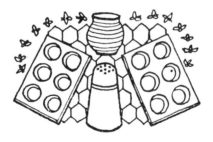

CACEN CNEIFIO
SHEARING CAKE

(A cake prepared for shearing time).

½ lb. flour (plain)
6 ozs. moist sugar
4 ozs. butter
Rind of ½ lemon
1 egg
¼ pint milk
1 teaspoonful baking-powder
2 teaspoonfuls carraway seeds
Little grated nutmeg

Rub butter into flour, mix all dry ingredients together and then stir in the milk and beaten egg. Bake in a greased cake tin lined with buttered paper, in a moderate oven for one hour.

Oven Control, Mark 6

WELSH CURD CAKES

1 pint firmly set junket   *½ oz. cake crumbs*
2 ozs. margarine   *Rind of lemon*
Yolks of 2 eggs   *1 teaspoonful brandy*
½ oz. sugar   *Pinch of salt*
½ oz. currants

Cut junket and drain through muslin to remove whey, cream butter and sugar, add eggs, crumbs, flavouring and curds. Fill into patty tins lined with short pastry. Bake in moderate oven for 15-20 minutes.

Oven Control, Mark 6

TEISEN DROS-NOS
OVER-NIGHT CAKE

½ *lb. flour*
4 *ozs. fat*
3-4 *ozs. sugar*
Mixed dry fruit
1 *teaspoonful cinnamon*
1 *teaspoonful ginger*
½ *teaspoonful bicarbonate of soda*
1 *tablespoonful vinegar*
Milk

Rub fat to flour and add rest of dry ingredients. Mix with milk to a fairly soft consistency. Quickly mix the bicarbonate of soda with the vinegar and stir into the mixture thoroughly. Leave batter overnight and bake next day in a lined and greased tin for 1-1¼ hours in a moderate oven.

Oven Control, Mark 5

FARMHOUSE DRIPPING CAKE

12 *ozs. plain flour*
3 *rounded teaspoonfuls baking-powder*
6 *ozs. dripping*
2 *ozs. butter or margarine*
6 *ozs. brown sugar*
4 *ozs. currants*
4 *ozs. sultanas*
¼ *teaspoonful nutmeg*
1 *egg*
1 *gill milk*
Pinch of salt

Sift flour, salt, nutmeg and baking-powder together. Rub fat into flour. Add fruit and sugar. Mix well but lightly with beaten egg and milk. Turn into tin and bake in a moderate oven for 1½ hours.

Oven Control, Mark 5

FARMHOUSE LARD CAKE

1 *lb. bread dough*	2 *ozs. lemon peel*
8 *ozs. lard*	2 *ozs. sugar*
4 *ozs. currants*	

Turn dough on to floured paste-board and roll out until it is about an inch thick; spread 2 ozs. of lard on the dough with 2 ozs. currants and 1 oz. lemon peel, sift over it a little flour and sugar; fold dough over, roll out again and put another 2 ozs. lard, 2 ozs. currants and 1 oz. peel. Repeat the rolling and larding until dough has been rolled out four times.

Handle dough lightly and do not press heavily upon it with rolling pin. Bake in a well-greased tin in a moderate oven about one hour. Serve in squares (hot or cold) with butter.

Oven Control, Mark 6

CHEESE MUFFINS

1½ *cupfuls flour (plain)*
½ *cupful grated cheese*
¼ *teaspoonful salt*
4 *teaspoonfuls baking-powder*
1 *egg*
¾ *cupful milk*

Beat the egg lightly, add the salt and milk. Sift flour and baking-powder together, and then put in the grated cheese. Make into a dough with the liquid, beat well and roll out. Cut into rounds, brush with beaten egg, and bake for 10 minutes in a sharp oven. They are delicious split, spread with butter and eaten hot or cold, preferably hot.

Oven Control, Mark 7

TEISEN REIS GREIDDELL
RICE GIRDLE CAKES

1 *teacupful boiled rice*
1 *teacupful flour*
1 *teacupful milk*
1 *tablespoonful butter*
1 *teaspoonful salt*
2 *teaspoonfuls baking-powder*
1 *egg*

Mix together rice, melted butter, salt and well-beaten egg. Sieve together baking-powder and flour, add to mixture and stir well. Drop large tablespoonfuls on to hot greased bakestone or thick frying-pan. Cook about four minutes each side.

These are delicious served very hot with golden syrup.

CAERPHILLY SCONES

1½ *ozs. butter*
¾ *lb. flour*
3 *teaspoonfuls baking-powder*
¼ *teaspoonful salt*
Pepper to taste
3 *ozs. Caerphilly Cheese*
2 *ozs. Parmesan*
About ½ pint milk

Sift flour, salt, baking-powder, rub in butter. Grate cheese finely, add to flour with pinch of pepper. Mix well, add enough milk to make soft dough. Roll out half inch thick, stamp into rounds, place on buttered baking sheet. Bake in hot oven 15 or 20 minutes. Serve hot with butter.

Oven Control, Mark 7

46

TEISEN DE HEN FAMGU
GREAT-GRANDMOTHER'S TEA CAKE

½ *lb. flour*
1 *teaspoonful baking-powder*
3 *ozs. butter*
3 *tablespoonfuls milk*
1 *egg*
3 *ozs. sugar*
Pinch of salt
3 *tablespoonfuls of sherry*

Rub butter into flour, add sugar, baking-powder and salt. Beat egg well and add milk and sherry. Stir this liquid into other ingredients.

Bake in shallow tin for about 20 minutes in a moderate oven. Serve hot, well buttered.

Oven Control, Mark 5

TEISEN CNAU A FFRWYTHAU
FRUIT AND NUT CAKE

½ *lb. self-raising flour*
3 *ozs. brown sugar*
1 egg
½ *lb. stoned dates*
3 *ozs. of shelled walnuts*
¾ *of a cupful of boiling water*
½ *teaspoonful of bicarbonate of soda*
½ *teaspoonful of salt*

Chop dates and walnuts and to these add the bicarbonate and the salt. Then pour on the boiling water and leave for two minutes. Add sugar. Then the flour and lastly the well-beaten egg.

Bake in a moderate oven for about one hour. Cut and spread with margarine or butter.

Oven Control, Mark 5

TEISEN DDU NADOLIG
CHRISTMAS CAKE

The old folks used home-brew to mix the cake, but our Cardigan reader assures us that pale ale will serve as well. She also adds the warning that although a bottle of pale ale is included in the ingredients all of this should not be used if the mixture appears to be getting too soft.

1½ lbs. flour
½ lb. butter (or margarine)
1 lb. castor sugar
¼ lb. mixed peel
½ lb. currants
½ lb. raisins
½ lb. sultanas
4 ozs. sweet almonds
Half a nutmeg grated
½ oz. yeast
Mixed spice (if wished)
Bottle of pale ale
Juice of half an orange and half a lemon

Rub yeast into flour, when well mixed rub in the fat, sugar, fruit and spices, add fruit juices, mix with pale ale. Do not allow mixture to become too soft. Bake in a moderate oven for three hours.

Oven Control, Mark 5

48

A TASTY SALAD DRESSING

1 *egg*
1 *tablespoonful sugar*
Dash of pepper and salt
1 *teaspoonful mustard*
1 *tablespoonful melted butter*
1 *dessertspoonful flour*
½ *teacupful milk*
½ *teacupful vinegar*
½ *teacupful warm water*

Mix egg, sugar, salt, pepper together. Add flour and mustard; keep it a nice smooth paste. Add melted butter, milk, water and, lastly, vinegar.

Cook over a small heat until as thick as cream, but do not boil.

APPLE GINGER

4 *lbs. apples*   3 *lemons*
2 *lbs. granulated sugar* 2 *ozs. ginger*
4 *lbs. lump sugar*   ½ *teaspoonful cayenne pepper*

Peel and core the apples and quarter. Make syrup from 2 lbs. granulated sugar in a pint of water. Let it boil, then pour over the apples. Let it stand for two days. Add 4 lbs. of lump sugar, the rind and juice of the three lemons. Add the ginger (after bruising in a bag). Add the cayenne, let it all boil until the juice is clear. Simmer about one hour.

GOOSEBERRY MINT JELLY

2 lbs. gooseberries (green)
About six stalks of fresh mint
Sugar

Place gooseberries in a preserving pan, just cover with cold water and cook until soft. Strain carefully and to each pint of liquid add 1 lb. of sugar. Replace in the preserving pan, together with the mint tied up in a bundle. Heat gently till the sugar is melted, then boil until it "jells". Remove the mint, pour into glass jars and seal.

LOSHIN DU
TREACLE TOFFEE

½ lb. treacle (syrup)   *1 tablespoonful butter*
½ lb. demerara sugar

Melt butter in a saucepan, then add treacle and sugar. Stir gently. Boil until a few drops poured into cold water set crisp (about 10 minutes). Pour into rectangular greased tin. When nearly cold cut into sizeable squares. Nuts may be added if liked.

SURYN CYFFAITH POETH

Unusual recipe for a Welsh sauce which should be served with veal.

6 *lemons*	¼ *oz. mace*
2 *ozs. horseradish*	¼ *oz. nutmeg*
1 *lb. salt*	¼ *oz. cayenne*
6 *cloves of garlic*	2 *ozs. mustard*
¼ *oz. cloves*	2 *quarts of malt vinegar*

Cut the lemons into eighths and cover with salt, cut the horseradish very finely, then place with the rest of the ingredients in a big jar that has a lid. Place the jar in a boiler of water (with the water coming to within two inches of the rim of the jar). Bring to the boil and boil for 15 minutes. Stir the mixture every day for six weeks, and keep the lid on. At the end of six weeks strain into small bottles and cork tightly. This will keep for years, and a little will go far. Serve with veal.

HOME-MADE WINES

GWIN MWYAR DUON
BLACKBERRY WINE

6 *lbs. blackberries*   4 *lbs. white sugar*
1 *gallon of boiling water*   ½ *oz. yeast*

Pour the boiling water on to the blackberries. Stir well, night and morning for two days. Strain. Dissolve the sugar in the liquid and add the yeast. Stir.

X Pour the sweetened yeasted liquid into a clean cask, jar or bottle (depending on the quantity) until it is filled to the top. Keep any surplus in a bottle for topping up the water receptacle during fermentation. Stand the cask (or jar or bottle) on a tray in a warm room. Fermentation soon begins and froth will pour out over the side of the container. Fill up again from the surplus bottle until a froth no longer forms. Insert a cork into the container, loosely at first, but when the fermentation is over and no bubbles of gas are seen, then cork tightly. If you want a really clear wine it should be racked from time to time, i.e. pour the clear wine from the old bottles, into clean ones, keeping the yeast deposit to re-clear in the old bottles.

The wine should be kept for six months without sampling **X**.

From **X** to **X** is the method used for most wines.

GWIN DANT Y LLEW
DANDELION WINE

3 quarts of dandelion flowers, picked when dry

Pour over them, 1 gallon of boiling water. Cover with a thick
cloth, and allow to stand for 24 hours, stirring night and
morning. Strain, and to every gallon of liquid add 3 lbs. of
sugar, the juice and rind of 2 lemons or 2 oranges (but none
of the white pith). Boil for 30 minutes. Let it cool and then
add ½ oz. yeast on a piece of toasted bread. Let it float on the
surface. Allow it to ferment for 3 or 4 days. Strain, and then
proceed as between **X** and **X** in the previous recipe.

GWIN GWENITH, NEU WIN TATWS
WHEAT OR POTATO WINE

2 lbs. old potatoes, unpeeled, cut up small
2 lbs. raisins – split
1 lb. washed wheat
4 lbs. demerara sugar
1 gallon boiling water
1 oz. yeast

Pour the boiling water on to the other ingredients and stir
well. When cool, add the yeast and cover for 14 days, stirring
night and morning. Strain, and then proceed from **X** as before.

This should be kept for 12 months.

GWIN YSGAW
ELDERBERRY WINE

Add a pint of berries to a pint of water, and a little pickling spice placed in a small bag. Boil for 20 minutes, stirring and bruising the fruit. Strain. To every quart of liquid add 1 lb. of lump sugar. When cool add 1½ ozs. yeast to every gallon, allowing the yeast to float on a piece of toast. Leave to ferment for 10 days. Stirring twice a day. The proceed from **X** as before.

(Alternative method).

7 lbs. elderberries (stripped and stalked)
3 lbs. loaf sugar
1 lb. seedless raisins
½ oz. ground ginger

6 cloves
½ oz. yeast
3 gallons boiling water

Place berries in large vessel and cover with boiling water and leave for 24 hours. Mash fruit and strain through a jelly-bag. Put in a preserving pan, add sugar, ginger, raisins and cloves. Boil slowly for one hour, skimming all the time. Let liquid cool and add yeast. Pour into an earthenware vessel and leave for two weeks to ferment. Bottle and cork and let wine stand for at least three months.

PARSNIP WINE

4 lbs. chopped unpeeled parsnips to each gallon of water

Boil, but do not let the parsnips turn into a mash or the wine will be cloudy. Strain carefully, but do not squeeze. To each gallon, add 3 lbs. white sugar. Boil for ½ hour. Add the juice of 1 lemon and 1 orange and when cool add the yeast on toast – ½ oz. yeast to the gallon. Allow to stand in a warm place, and when fermentation starts, proceed from **X** as before.

GWIN BLODYN YSGAW
ELDER FLOWER WINE

There are two methods:

(1)   1 *pint of flowers only with no green stalks*
          3 *lbs. sugar*
          3 *lemons*
          1 *gallon cold water*

Put all these ingredients in a pan, cover with the cloth and stand for a fortnight, stirring every day. Then proceed from **X** as before.

(2)   1 *pint of flowers*
          1 *quart cold water*

Boil for 20 minutes and strain. Add 1 lb. sugar, 1 orange and 1 lemon to every quart of liquid. When cool, add the yeast on a piece of toast, allowing ½ oz. of yeast to a gallon. Then proceed from **X** as before.

PARSLEY WINE

1 *lb. parsley – leaves, no stalks*
2 *oranges*
2 *lemons*
4 *lbs. demerara sugar*
1 *gallon water*
Yeast

Put the parsley in a muslin bag with the lemon and orange rinds. Pour the water over it and bring to the boil. Simmer for half an hour. Squeeze the bag and remove from the pan. Add the sugar (4 lbs. to the gallon) and the fruit juices. When cool add the yeast (½ oz. to the gallon) and proceed from **X** as before.

RHUBARB WINE

5 *lbs. rhubarb*	1 *lb. raisins*
4 *lbs. sugar*	1 *gallon*
Juice of 2 lemons	

Cut up the rhubarb, unpeeled, into small pieces. Place in a pan and add the water. Let it stand for a week to soften. Strain and add the sugar, juice and raisins. If a very clear wine is required add ¼ oz. isinglass dissolved in a little warm water. Stir every day and when it ceases to "work" bottle it, but do not cork tightly till the "hissing" has stopped.

NETTLE AND BURDOCK DRINK

2 *quarts of nettles*	2 *lbs. sugar*
2 *ozs. hops*	1 *lemon*
2 *ozs. burdock*	2 *ozs. yeast*
6 *quarts water*	

Boil nettles, hops and burdock slowly for half-an-hour. Strain, add sugar and cut up lemon. Leave till lukewarm. Put the yeast, spread on round of toasted bread, on top of brew. Leave for 12 hours. Bottle and make airtight. Can be used in 12 hours.

GWIN DANADL POETHION
NETTLE SYRUP

Gather the tops of young nettles, wash well, and to every 1 lb. of nettles add one quart of water. Boil for one hour, strain, and to every pint of juice add 1lb. sugar. Boil for 30 minutes, and when cold bottle. This syrup is said to have great health-giving powers as a blood-purifier.

Used with soda water it is a cooling drink.

GWIN LLYGAD Y DYDD
DAISY WINE

4 quarts of the small field daisy blossoms
1 gallon boiling water
2 lemons
2 oranges
2 lbs. brown sugar
½ lb. raisins
1 oz. yeast

Put the daisies in a bowl and cover with boiling water. Stand until next day, then squeeze daisies out. Boil with sliced lemons, oranges, and sugar for 20 minutes. Allow to cool to lukewarm. Add chopped raisins and stir the yeast in (it should be first dissolved in a little warm water). Leave to ferment 14 days. Then skim, strain, and bottle.

GWIN BRIALLU
PRIMROSE WINE

2 *quarts primrose petals* 3 *lbs. sugar*
1 *gallon cold water* 1 *lb. wheat*
1 *lb. raisins* 1 *oz. yeast*

Put the primroses into the water and leave eight days, then squeeze them out. Put the chopped raisins, sugar and wheat into the liquid and stir until the sugar is dissolved, then sprinkle the yeast on top and leave to ferment 28 days. Skim, strain and bottle.

GWIN BRIALLU MAIR neu
GWIN SAWDL Y FUWCH
COWSLIP WINE

25 *lbs. loaf sugar* *Yeast*
9 *seville oranges* 1 *quart brandy*
9 *gallons cowslip flowers*

To make nine gallons of wine, boil for half an hour nine gallons of water with 25 lbs. of loaf preserving sugar and leave for 36 hours. Then put into a tub the juice and peel of nine Seville oranges and nine gallons of cowslip flowers or pips, over these put the sugar and water and leave them to stand for about four days, stirring daily.

Afterwards strain, add a quart of brandy, put the wine into a cask, leave for two months, then bottle it.

GWIN DAIL DERW
OAK LEAF WINE

For each gallon:

A quanity of clean brown withered oak leaves
gathered from the tree on a dry day
Bruised piece of whole ginger
4 lbs. white sugar
1 lb. chopped raisins
½ oz. yeast

Place the leaves in a china or earthenware vessel and pour sufficient boiling water over them to cover. Infuse for 4 to 5 days, then strain off through muslin. Boil this liquid, adding a bruised piece of whole ginger and 4 lbs. of sugar. After 20 minutes boiling allow to cool to lukewarm and return to the earthenware vessel. Now add the 1 lb. of chopped raisins and ½ oz. of yeast. Cover well and allow to ferment for 16 days, then strain and bottle. The wine will be ready to drink in three months, but improves with keeping.

GWIN PWMPEN
PUMPKIN WINE

Take a large pumpkin, extract the seeds and pulp and place the pumpkin in a large jar or suitable vessel.

Fill the cavity with granulated sugar, cover with a cloth and stand in a warm place. Each day add more sugar until the pumpkin has completely dissolved. Then strain the liquor, add the juice of two lemons and for each quart of liquid add ¼ pint rum. Pour into bottles immediately and cork tightly. Keep this beverage for six months before using.

BEETROOT WINE

7 lbs. beetroot (washed and diced)
3¾ lbs. sugar
1 lb. raisins
1 oz. stick ginger
½ oz. cloves
½ oz. yeast
7 quarts water
1 lemon
White of 1 egg

Place the beetroot in a large vesel with the water and boil for one hour. Mash and strain the beetroot. Put back to boil with the raisins, ginger, cloves and half the sugar. Boil for 15 minutes. Remove from the fire, add remainder of sugar plus the juice and rind of one lemon.

Let the liquid cool and put in large earthenware vessel. Add the yeast on a slice of toast. Cover and leave for three days.

Strain the wine and stir well. Add the white of an egg, stir, and remove scum from the top of the wine daily for 10-14 days. Bottle, cork, and store in a cool place for at least three months before using.

DIOD DAIL
HERB BEER

A good dozen nettle-tops
About 1 oz. dandelion leaves
1 oz. root ginger
1 lb. demerara sugar
½ oz. yeast

Tie bruised ginger in muslin and boil with herbs in one gallon of cold water for about half an hour. Strain on to sugar and stir well. When lukewarm put in yeast floating on a piece of toast. Stand overnight and bottle next day in corked bottles. Ready to drink after two or three days.

MEDD HEN FFASIWN
MEAD

Ingredients:

Honey, hops, ginger, allspice

To every gallon of water allow 4 lbs. of honey and for a hogs-head allow ½ lb. hops, ¾ lb. bruised ginger and ¼ lb. allspice.

The honey and water should first be boiled for one hour, and skimmed, then the spices added, and boiled for about 10 minutes. As it will probably be inconvenient to boil enough to fill a hogshead, put part into the cask, and fill up every day until the cask is full.

Having boiled the liquor, strain it, add the yeast on toast, and let it remain two days; then skim it off, and put the liquor in the barrel; when the cask is full, and the mead has finished fermenting bung it down closely. Bottle in a year.

DIOD SINSIR
WELSH GINGER BEER

Take a 10-pint saucepan half-filled with dandelions and nettles in equal proportions, together with two sticks of rhubarb, and four sticks of ginger, which have previously been pounded.

Fill up with cold water. Boil all together for about 15 minutes, together with a handful of currant leaves. Then strain and add 1 lb. of white sugar to the liquid. Stir, and add eight pints of cold water.

When lukewarm, mix one ounce of yeast in a cup of the liquid and add it to the remainder. Leave overnight. In the morning skim off the yeast and bottle the liquid, but do not cork tightly at first.

CWRW BACH
ALE – STRONG AND SMALL BEER

Boil together for half an hour 10 pints water, 3 doz. dandelions, 3 doz. nettles, 6 sticks ginger pounded, 3 sticks rhubarb, some currant tops, 2 large handfuls hops.

Strain and add 1 lb. demerara sugar; stir, add 6 pints cold water; when lukewarm sprinkle over surface 1 oz. yeast.

Leave overnight, skin and bottle.

Country people add a sprig of wormwood, which is considered to be a good tonic.

GWIN EIRIN DUON
DAMSON PORT

4 *lbs. damsons*   1 *gallon boiling water*
4 *lbs. sugar*

Pour the boiling water over the damsons and leave them 10 days, stirring and squeezing them each day. Then run through a jelly bag and afterwards strain twice without squeezing. This will save a lot of wine later.

Add the sugar to the strained liquid and stir until it is dissolved. Add a teacupful of boiling water to raise the temperature and leave to ferment 14 days. Skim and bottle, corking very loosely.

GWIN AFALAU
APPLE WINE

4 quarts of apples
1 gallon boiling water
2 lemons
Piece of bruised ginger
A few cloves
Sugar

Crush apples, pour over boiling water, cover with cloth and leave for fortnight, squeezing daily. Strain, add cloves and bruised ginger and measure, allowing ½ lb. sugar to each pint of liquor. Add juice of lemons, stir well until sugar has dissolved. Leave to stand until a scum has formed on surface. Skim, pour into bottles, and tie corks down securely.